The Constitution

v.

Murphy's Law

by Byron Winter

The
Constitution
v.
Murphy's Law

ISBN-13: 978-1543161120
ISBN-10: 154316112X

Printed by CreateSpace

Available on Amazon.com

Cover art by the author

Table of Contents

Page

Introduction:
Law 101

Back when our country was young, Alexis de Toqueville toured the country and found that he could have intelligent discussions on law and government even in the small towns. Today, this isn't so. Very few people have taken the time to read their State Constitution, the Federalist Papers, or even one Supreme Court decision. So, to help the reader understand this book, here are four words and five undisputed legal facts that we will need as a foundation:

- "Venue" means place: There are two: one of the 50 States and one of D.C. and the territories.
- "Jurisdiction" means type of court. In Britain there were four types of courts: Law, Equity (Chancery), Admiralty, and Maritime. They were in different court houses with different judges. In America, we put all the jurisdictions in one court house and in front of one judge. So, it is reasonable to ask the judge what his jurisdiction is, but as you will see, today's judges will not answer the question.
- "Positive Law": Acts passed by Congress and found in the US Statutes at Large (which are not organized by subject matter) **or** Acts collected and revised by Congress, sorted by subject matter into a Title of the US Code, then, the whole Title is passed as an Act of Congress. About half of the Titles of the US Code are positive law. The rest are:
- Prima facia Law": The current acts of Congress collected, organized, and published by private

publishing companies; sometimes with mistakes.
- Congress can create courts in every branch of government. Judicial courts uphold the Constitution, but Legislative and Executive branch "courts" cannot and do not uphold it.

"Legislative courts are but agencies in drag. . ." *Karst, Federal Jurisdiction Haiku, 32 Stan. L. Rev. 229,230 (1979)*

- There are two types of citizenship: State and Federal. Every provision of the Constitution and the Bill of Rights protects a State citizen. A Federal citizen has no Bill of Rights and only has a vague right to property and due process of law. A Federal citizen is also called a 14th Amendment citizen.
- Examples of Court case numbers:
  - Supreme Court- 100 US 200, 210, 1937. 100 is the volume, 200 is the page where the case starts and 210 is the page where the quotation is.
  - Circuit Court/ US Court of Appeals- 300 F. 2nd 400. "F" is for Federal Reporter.
  - District Court of the United States/ US District Court- 500 F. Supp 600. "F Supp" is for Federal Supplement.
- United States Code- Title 44, section 3512 is written (44 USC 3512). US Statutes at Large- 62 Stat 898 means volume 62, chapter 898.

I have to prove everything, so this book will be like a toned down legal brief, but without the Latin words, needless words (obiter dicta), and dishonest arguments so common to Supreme Court decisions.

Primary source materials

available on www.commonsensemurphy.com)

80th CONGRESS
1st Session **H. R. 3214**

IN THE SENATE OF THE UNITED STATES

JULY 8 (legislative day, JULY 7), 1947
Read twice and referred to the Committee on the Judiciary

AN ACT

To revise, codify, and enact into law title 28 of the United States Code entitled "Judicial Code and ̄ ̄iciary".

Be it enacted by the Senate and House o. ̧ ̧presentatives of the United States of America in Congress ae̊ ̧ ̧.ed, That title 28 of the United States Code, entitled "Judicial Code and Judiciary" is hereby revi ̧ ̧ ̄ odified, and enacted into law, and may be cited as "Title 28, United States Code, section —", as follows:

TITLE 28, JUDICIARY AND JUDICIAL PROCEDURE

JUDICIAL CODE AND JUDICIARY

HEARINGS

BEFORE A

SUBCOMMITTEE OF THE
COMMITTEE ON THE JUDICIARY
UNITED STATES SENATE

EIGHTIETH CONGRESS

SECOND SESSION

ON

H. R. 3214

AN ACT TO REVISE, CODIFY, AND ENACT INTO LAW
TITLE 28 OF THE UNITED STATES CODE
ENTITLED "JUDICIAL CODE AND
JUDICIARY"

APRIL 22, 23, 24, AND 26, AND JUNE 7, 1948

Printed for the use of the Committee on the Judiciary

vii

Chapter 1

Constitutional Holes

The idea that there is a constitutional way to evade the Constitution seems impossible, but this book will prove otherwise. There are many details of governing which the Constitution leaves out and which can be used to get around most of that Charter. I call them holes.

Hole #1
The Constitution only requires the existence of one court: the Supreme Court.

"The judicial Power of the United States, shall be vested in one supreme Court, and in such inferior Courts as the Congress may from time to time ordain and establish." *Const., Art. III, sec. 1.*

"Shall" is required and "may" is optional. No other Federal court below the Supreme Court needs to exist and it would be perfectly legal. The Judiciary Act of 1801 abolished two District Courts. and the Judiciary Act of 1802 abolished six Circuit Courts.

Hole #2
The Constitution does not reserve the words "judge", "judicial", or "court" exclusively for Article III judges and courts. Congress has used two provisions of the Constitution to create courts in both the legislative and executive branches of the Federal government. Article IV, section 3 gives Congress the power to make "all needed Rules and Regulations respecting the Territory or other Property belonging to the United States;" and

1

by direct implication, territorial courts to hear cases stemming from those rules and regulations. Article I, section 8 gives Congress the power "To make all Laws which shall be necessary and proper for carrying into Execution the foregoing Powers,". From this provision, Congress has made "Boards" and "Courts" in both the Executive and Legislative branches.

"In the Williams case, the Supreme Court said that (if) a duty was to be performed, if a function was to be accomplished, a purpose was to be served. Congress could determine how it was to be done, it could determine that it be done judicially, and could put such a judicial duty on an executive, and an administrator, or it could say 'we will have it done by a legislative court.'"

Hon. Bolon Turner, presiding judge, Tax Court of the United States, Senate Hearing for H.R. 3214, pg. 288, 1948. (Parenthesis mine)

"when Congress decided that it would not put the power to perform the particular function administratively, but judicially, then it hereby would create a legislative court, and that is distinguished from the general judicial powers contemplated by the Constitution which under Article III must be placed in the constitutional courts." *Ibid at 282*

I'm sure you noticed the confusing language. Judge Turner saying that an executive or legislative branch Board or "court" could act judicially. He went on to explain that he considered his Tax Court judicial, rather than administrative because it had no power to make policy, as do the Interstate Commerce Commission, the

Federal Communication Commission, or the Federal Trade Commission. Rather, the Tax Court just heard evidence and made decisions which Judge Turner considers "acting judicially". Even the Supreme Court is guilty of using loose language. In US v. Union Pacific RR Co., *98 US 569, 603,* the Supreme Court said the Court of Claims was a constitutional court (Article III), in part because the judges had life tenure. Later in Ex parte Bakelite Corp'n, *279 US 438,* it decided the court was a legislative court (Article I), even if the judges did have life tenure.

Hole #3

Not only can Congress create courts, it can rename them and change their branch of government. Prior to 1942, Tax Court was named the Board of Tax Appeals.

"The Customs Court was the Board of General Appraisers, and there is no question about it. It came under the Customs Code; in 1928 a bill was introduced to change its name from Board of General Appraisers to the Customs Court. . . . In 1939, however, a bill was introduced to do exactly in the case of the Customs Court what H.R. 3214 does in respect to the Tax Court. It moved it into the judiciary*,"

Hon. Bolon Turner, presiding judge, Tax Court of the United States, Senate Hearing for H.R. 3214, pg. 286, 1948.

*The judge is speaking loosely again, he means the court moved to the legislative branch, and there was acting judicially. Tax Court is not and has never been in the Judicial branch of government.

Hole #4

The Constitution does not make restrictions on how Federal officers may or may not be moved between the different branches of government. Currently, once a proposed officer gets nominated by the President and approved by the Senate, he does not have to be re-vetted if he is moved into another ranch of government as long as he is doing a similar job.

"It cannot be doubted, and has frequently been the case, that Congress may increase the power and duties of an existing office without thereby rendering it necessary that the incumbent should be again nominated and appointed." *Shoemaker v. U.S., 147 US 282, 301, 1893.*

Hole #5

Nothing in the Constitution requires the Congress to be a good bookkeeper of the Law.

"Federal statute laws are drafted in perhaps a majority of instances without any reference whatsoever to existing law. In many cases they contain provisions which are inconsistent with or duplicate existing law, but do not specifically repeal the existing law, nor directly amend it. . . . a total of more than 70 books (of the US Statutes at Large) to which recourse would have to be had to ascertain the present status of a law enacted in 1873."*Charles Zinn, Law Revision Counsel, House Comm. on the Judiciary, Senate Hearings for H.R. 3214, pg. 331-332, 1948. (parenthesis mine)*

"Senator Donnell: Are you able to tell us, Judge, whether the practitioner in the smaller towns and cities of the country generally has adequate library facilities to enable him to go back to the original sources (US Statutes at Large or the Revised Statutes of 1873) which you have mentioned?
Judge Albert Maris, (Cir. Ct. of Appeals): Mr. Chairman, I will go further, and include in that list the United States district judges in a lot of districts throughout the country." *Senate Hearings for H.R. 3214, pg. 31, 1948.(parenthesis mine)*

This poor house keeping also applies to changes with the Federal courts. Congress fails to officially abolish the courts that it transforms.

Judge Maris: "This amendment, however, will make it clear beyond any doubt that the bill does not abolish the old courts and create successor courts but rather continues all the existing courts, including those of which the names are slightly changed, without interruption of powers, jurisdiction or proceedings pending therein." *Senate Hearings for H.R. 3214, pg. 28, 1948*

and

" Senator Donnell: . . . the bill (HR 3214) does not abolish the existing independent agency in the executive branch of government now known as the Tax Court of the United States, but merely converts it into a legislative court?
Judge Turner: "Exactly; yes.
Senator Donnell: What disposition would be made of

5

cases now pending before the presently existing Tax Court? I take it your answer is they would continue right along.

 Judge Turner: There would be no hiatus, no dismissal of those cases, but they would be merely handled in the future by the court rather than by the administrative agency, . . ." above, *Senate Hearings for H.R. 3214, pgs. 286, 1948. (parenthesis mine)*

Chapter 2

1934 - 1948

The Federal courts began to go through big changes in 1934, beginning with the Rules Enabling Act of March 8, 1934 *(48 Stat. 399).* In this act, Congress gave the "authority" to prescribe the rules and procedures for criminal cases to the US Supreme Court. This was soon followed by an act which, likewise, did the same for civil cases. *(48 Stat. 1064, June 19, 1934).*

Authorizing the Supreme Court to write rules and procedures for the Federal courts is simply not one of Congress' enumerated powers as spelled out in Article I, sec. 8 of the Constitution. It seems to violate separation of powers. Still, the Supreme Court supports the idea, but what it used as support is ridiculous. In *Sibbach v. Wilson & Co., 312 US 1,9-10; (1941),* citing *Wayman v. Southard, 23 US 1,4 (1825),* the Court quotes the writings of Sir Edward Coke, (died 1633), who commented on the writings of Sir Thomas Littleton, (died 1481). Specifically, the Court refers to Coke on Littleton, Section 58: TENANT FOR TERM OF YEARS.

"When Littleton wrote, many persons might make leases for years, or for life or lives, at their will and pleasure, who now cannot make them firm in law. And some persons may now make leases for years, or for life or lives (observing due incidents), firm and good in law, who of themselves could not do so when Littleton wrote, and this by force of divers acts of parliament; as

7

namely, 32 H. 8. 1 Eliz. 13Eliz. 18Eliz. and 1 Jac. Regis, of which statutes one is enabling, and the rest are disabling." *58 Coke on Littleton, (1630) (slightly edited for readability)*

So, the Supreme Court would have us believe that because this one English law was changed by Queen Elizabeth I and King James I, that Congress has the authority to authorize rules for American courts 300 years later. The Constitution says nothing about court rules, but the Federalist Papers come close to addressing the subject.

"The entire legislature can perform no judiciary act, though by the joint act of two of its branches the judges may be removed from their offices," *Federalist 47, Madison.*

and

"The members of the legislature will rarely be chosen with a view to those qualifications which fit men for the stations of judges; and as, on this account, there will be great reason to apprehend all the ill consequences of defective information, so, on account of the natural propensity of such bodies to party divisions, there will be no less reason to fear that the pestilential breath of faction may poison the fountains of justice." *Federalist 81, Hamilton.*

It is odd that the Supreme Court reached back to the 1600s when it could have noticed a more recent British statute; The Law Term Act of 1830. In chapter 70, section XI of this act, King George IV enabled the

British judges to write their own rules. Going even farther back in time, in response to the Star Chamber interrogations of Sir Nicholas Throchmorton (died 1571), it is clear English judges wrote their own rules. Specifically, they changed the rules of evidence to disallow forced confessions.

"The change in the English criminal procedure in that particular (confessions) seems to be founded upon no statute and no judicial opinion, but upon the general and silent acquiescence of the courts in a popular demand." (cites omitted) *Miranda v. Arizona, 394 US 438, 443, (1966) (parenthesis mine)*

The Supreme Court also overlooked its own 1911 Rule Book which begins with:

3.

Practice

"This court considers the former practice of the courts of king's bench and of chancery, in England, as affording outline for the practice of this court; and will, from time to time make such alterations therein as circumstances may render necessary."

This rule book also gave limited direction to the district courts. It appears the Supreme Court decided to give Congress the power to authorize court rules and then went looking for support, however thin that support was. Letting Congress authorize rules for the courts changed the balance of power between the Federal government and the several States. The Judiciary Act of 1789, *(1 Stat. 73, September 24, 1789)* required Federal courts to conform, as much as possible, with the rules of whichever State they were located. Consequently,

Legislative courts are but agencies in drag.

there was no single book of Federal Court Rules prior to 1948. Not likely did anyone feel the need to define the word "State", but that will change with the new rules.

Hopefully, this long discussion of the history of judges writing their own rules has shown the reader that the Supreme Court opinions do not deserve your confidence. The justices of the Supreme Court criticize each other for only knowing the historical facts that help their current argument. Be prepared to read more garbage decisions of the Supreme Court.

After Congress authorized the writing of court rules, committees were formed, work done, acts were amended, everything was approved by Congress, and finally the rules become effective. The civil rules became effective on Sept. 16, 1938. The criminal rules, likewise, on March 21, 1946.

At this time, the workhorses of the Federal court system were the District Courts of the United States; these courts were below the Supreme Court under Article III of the Constitution. Article III, section 2 authorizes these courts to hear the following types of cases:

    1. To all cases of Law and Equity under:
- The Constitution
- The Laws of the United States
- Treaties

    2. To cases affecting:
- Ambassadors, Ministers, and Consuls

    3. Controversies between:
- Two or more States
- A State and Citizens of another State
- Citizens of different States
- Citizens of the same State claiming Lands

Legislative courts are but agencies in drag.
under Grants of different States
- A State or its Citizen and a foreign States, Citizens or Subjects

Please notice that there is no mention of the territories. Judicial courts cannot operate in those places which is why Congress had to create legislative courts in the first place. There is a long and complicated history of the courts of the District of Columbia. It ends up that it doesn't matter if D.C. is treated like a State or a territory. A legislative court is a legislative court no matter where it is.

For the District Courts of the United States to operate using rules authorized by Congress, instead of the State where they were located, put them in an awkward position. This is because the new Federal Rules of Criminal Procedure and the new Civil Rules each created definitions for the word "State".

Federal Rules of Criminal Procedure:
Rule 1, paragraph 9
"State" includes the District of Columbia, and any commonwealth, territory, or possession of the United States."

Civil Rule
Chapter 85 District Courts; Jurisdiction
Section 1332. Diversity of Citizenship; amount in controversy
(3)(b) The word "States", as used in this section, includes the Territories and the District of Columbia."
HR 3214, above. This definition is now 28 USC 1332 (e) and the Commonwealth of Puerto Rico has been added to the rule.

Legislative courts are but agencies in drag.

These definitions don't mention any of the several States. They only apply to places of "exclusive Federal jurisdiction" where the Bill of Rights does not apply.

Forgive me a small lesson in statutory construction; I will try to keep it as painless as possible. It is critically important to understand how to read legal definitions. First of all, realize that Congress' power to legislate is absolute. It can define the words in an act anyway it wants to and it can change definitions, at will, even in the same act. For example, in the current Social Security Act:

"Definitions
(b) For the purposes of this section----
        (1)the word 'State' does not mean the District of Columbia, Guam, or American Samoa, *42 USC 418."(Funding for Child Care)*

Compare this with the definition used in the original Social Security Act, (*49 Stat. 620, Aug. 7,1935)* and you will see they are opposites.

```
TITLE XI-GENERAL PROVISIONS
DEFINITIONS
SECTION 1101. (a) When used in this
Act-
(1) The term " State " (except when
used in section 531)includes Alaska,
Hawaii, and the District of Columbia.
(2) The term " United States " when
used in a geographical sense means
the States, Alaska, Hawaii, and the
District of Columbia.
```

The key word in the definitions is the word "includes" which the Supreme Court took pains to explain in Montello Salt Co. v. Utah.

"It (including) is the participle of the word 'include', which means, according to the Century Dictionary, (1) 'to confine within something; hold as an enclosure; to contain.' . . . The court (Supreme Court of Utah) also considered that the word 'including' was used as a word of enlargement, the learned court being of the opinion that such was its ordinary sense. With this we cannot concur. It is its exceptional sense, as the dictionaries and cases indicate." *Montello Salt Co. v. Utah 221 US 452 (1911) pgs. 465-466 (both parenthesis mine)*

In other words, "include" or "including" are words that set limits. The "rules" of statutory construction do allow a list to be expanded by "like kinds". But, the several States, where the Bill of Rights apply, is not like D.C. or the territories where it does not. The conclusion is that the new Federal Rules of Criminal Procedure (1948) and the Judicial Code (1948) are for D.C. and the territories, not for the several States.

Back to the time line. After the civil rules became effective in 1938 and before the passage of HR 3214 in 1948, the District Courts of the United States were judicial courts and legislative (territorial) courts, apparently, at the same time. This would not be the first time Congress had created a hybrid court. Judge Turner in explaining the difficulties faced by Tax Court described his own court as:

"an independent agency in the executive branch of the Government, charged only with judicial function, being (sic) in its present status being neither fish nor fowl," above, *Senate Hearings for H.R. 3214, pg. 295, 1948.*

13

This problem with the District Courts of the United States was resolved when President Truman signed into law HR. 3190 and H.R. 3214 on June 25, 1948. These acts revised, codified, and passed into positive law Title 18 (Crimes and Criminal Procedure) and Title 28 (Judiciary and Judicial Code) of the US Code. But HR 3214 did more; it created two new courts to operate using the new Titles 18 and 28 of the US Code.

> **§ 43. Creation and composition of courts**
> (a) There shall be in each circuit a court of appeals, which shall be a court of record, known as the United States Court of Appeals for the circuit.

> **§ 132. Creation and composition of district courts**
> (a) There shall be in each judicial district a district court which shall be a court of record known as the United States District Court for the district.

Because Congress can create "courts" for any branch of government, the question would be which branch are these new courts in? The Circuit Courts and the District Courts of the United States already existed in the judicial branch in 1948.

You don't create something you already have.

These courts, operating on rules authorized by Congress, with their venue and/or jurisdiction now changed to places of exclusive Federal jurisdiction due to Criminal Rule 1 (9) and Title 28, Section 1332 (3)(b), are legislative courts.

Legislative courts are but agencies in drag.
US District Court became the trial court of the Federal system, as it is remains today. If the Constitution does not apply there, it will not apply on appeal to the US Courts of Appeal or the Supreme Court. These higher courts are merely hearing an appeal from a lower legislative court decision, nothing more. It would not be an error if the Constitution was not upheld by the new courts. They can't even consider whether the laws passed by Congress are constitutional. They just uphold the will of Congress.

"Constitutional courts exercise the judicial power described in Article III of the Constitution; legislative courts do not and cannot." *Northern Pipeline Const. Co. v. Marathon Pipe Line Co., 458 US 50, 106 (1982) Justice White, dissenting).*

"Judge Turner: We (Tax Court) are the creature of Congress." *Senate Hearings for H.R. 3214, pg. 294, 1948.*

Being unrestrained by the Constitution, all of these judges can do almost anything. Sometimes, they pretend the Constitution applies, sometimes they don't, and sometimes they rewrite the law.

"Under all the usual rules of interpretation, in short, the Government should lose this case. But the normal rules of interpretation seem always to yield to the over-riding principle of the present Court: The Affordable Care Act must be saved." *King v. Burwell, 576 US ___, ___, slip op. At 2-3, 2015, pg. dissenting opinion, Justice Scalia.*

"It is bad enough for a court to cross out the words 'by

the State' once. But seven times?" *ibid.* at *6*

"Rather than rewriting the law under the pretense of interpreting it, the Court should have left it to Congress to decide what to do about the Act's limitations of tax credits to state exchanges." *ibid.* at *19*

One last point on the creation of the two new courts should be made. People seem to be under the impression that HR 3214 just changed the names of the Federal courts. But when Congress does that, it says so clearly:

CHAP. 411.—An Act To provide the name by which the Board of General Appraisers and members thereof shall hereafter be known.

May 28, 1926.
[H. R. 7566.]
[Public, No. 304.]

Be it enacted by the Senate and House of Representatives of the United States of America in Congress assembled, That the Board of General Appraisers shall hereafter be known as the United States Customs Court and the members thereof shall hereafter be known as the chief justice and the associate justices of the United States Customs Court.

Board of General Appraisers,
Known hereafter as United States Customs Court.
Vol. 26, p. 139.

Notice how Congress had to use this statute to also define the members as "justices" because they are not really judges.

Chapter 3

Step by step; hole by hole

The results of the passage of HR 3214, June 25, 1948:

a) The District Courts of the United States and the Circuit Courts of Appeal were abolished without any overt act of Congress. Hole #5.

b) This is lawful because the Constitution does not require any Article III court under the Supreme Court. Hole #1.

c) The US Courts of Appeal and US District Courts were created. Article IV, sec. 3 and Article I, sec. 8.

d) The judges and the pending cases of the abolished courts were moved into the Legislative branch, seamlessly. The judges did not have to be re-vetting. Hole #3 and Hole #4.

e) The judges were still called judges, they still had life tenure and their courts were still called courts. Hole #2 It is not unconstitutional to give legislative judges life tenure.

f) HR 3214 repealed the Conformity Acts. The new legislative courts, no longer had to conform to the rules and procedures of the State where they were located. Consequently, we now have one book of Federal Court Rules and State sovereignty is eroded.

g) Constitutional arguments are now outside the jurisdiction of the Federal Courts system for the average person.

h) Habeas Corpus is now dead, because it can only be based upon a violation of the Constitution.

i) The Constitution has been legally evaded.

Murphy's Law Wins.

Chapter 4

Summary of the Proof

US District Court and the US Court of Appeals are legislative courts." I have to fully prove this statement. So let me collect the facts shown in earlier chapters and add a few new facts which do prove it.

1. Both courts were "created" by HR 3214 in 1948. HR 3214 did not rename the courts.
2. Both courts can act in the territories; Judicial courts never could which is why legislative courts were created in the first place.
3. From the time of the first Judiciary Act of 1789 to the implementing of the new Civil Rules in 1938, the Federal Courts had to conform with the rules of whichever State they were located. Clearly, this was the original intent of the States when they ratified the Constitution. HR 3214 repealed the Conformity Acts which never applied to legislative courts anyway. The new Federal courts no longer have to conform with State rules and can use the new Federal Rules of Criminal and Civil Procedure.
4. The new Federal rules of Civil procedure merge Law and Equity. In the Constitution, Art. III, section 2, they are separate and distinct. What the Constitution separates, Congress cannot join; Constitution 101. This is more proof that US District Court is a legislative court where the Constitution does not apply.
5. The new Federal rules allow the judge to decide

19

a civil case without using the sitting jury (Civil Rule 50) or disregard/modify a jury verdict (Civil Rule 39, advisory juries)

6. Criminal Rule 29(c)(2) allows the judge to change the guilty verdict of a jury. All of which is contrary to the 6th and 7th Amendments. This could not happen in a court of Law and will be explained further in Chapter 7: The Aftermath.

7. Important cases are reported in the Federal Supplement or the Federal Reporter. In the volume where the Circuit Courts changed to US Courts of Appeal, 169 F 2nd, and the volume where the District Courts of the United States changed to US District Courts, 79 F. Supp., there is in each volume only one list of sitting judges. This shows that the judges moved seamlessly, into the new legislative courts.

8. In 1948, HR 3214 defines the words "judge" and "courts" to mean the courts and judges "constituted by Title 5" of the new Title 28 of the US Code. This wouldn't have been necessary if the judges and courts were judicial courts. But it was necessary because the new courts were actually agencies and the new judges weren't judicial at all.

9. The new legislative courts started reversing cases which had maintained Constitutional limits on Federal powers. This allowed the Federal government to expand beyond its enumerated powers and into Social Security, education, health care, the environment and more.

Chapter 5

Federal Judges

When Congress passed the Rules Enabling Act "authorizing" the Supreme Court to draft the criminal rules, civil rules, and rules of evidence; the Supreme Court could have said "No". If Congress wanted to create legislative courts, it would be fitting that Congress should write the rules to manage its creations. That's not what happened; the Supreme Court played along, as did the Federal judges. One wonders why?

After FDR had major initiatives of his New Deal programs struck down by the Circuit Courts and the Supreme Court, he threatened the Court with his infamous Court Packing Plan. The Plan would have expanded the Court to as many as 15 justices, all of whom would have been nominated by FDR. The threat was enough for two justices to change their minds and declare the Social Security Act and the National Labor Relations Act to be Constitutional. By 1943, seven of the Supreme Court justices were appointed by FDR. That probably explains the Court's acquiescence.

As far as the other Federal judges, it appears to be a different story. First of all, the changes were all constitutional. Still, these very capable judges must have known that the Constitution was being evaded. I looked to see if there was an increase in the number of judges retiring in protest in 1948 or thereafter. No. The number of US District Court judges retiring remained fairly constant at about 10% per year for 1948 +/- five years. Then I looked at the salaries for US District Court judges; *(source: Federal Judicial Center*

21

Effective Date	Annual Salary	% increase
Jan. 1, 1927	$10,000	33%
Aug. 1, 1946	$15,000	50%
Mar. 1, 1955	$22,500	50%
July 1, 1964	$30,000	33%
Mar. 1, 1969	$40,000	33%

The judges did get a healthy pay raise in 1946.

So what the district judges are doing is legal if you ignore the fact that they are "agencies in drag" and are still sending people to prison. To make it worse, they and the Supreme Court justices operate under a shroud of secrecy. I am not aware of any Federal court decision or Supreme Court opinion that identifies US District Court or the US Court of Appeals as being legislative courts; or Article III courts for that matter.

There is still one more piece of the puzzle:

Chapter 6

Federal Citizenship

US District Court is a legislative/territorial court, but most people don't live in D.C. or a territory; they live in one of the 50 States. It's not a problem when people file suit in Federal court because they do that voluntarily. This means they are voluntarily granting the court jurisdiction. The larger problem is when people are being dragged into Federal court to be prosecuted for a Federal crime. Using the power to define words, Congress has found a way to trick people into becoming Federal citizens which is sometimes called a 14th Amendment citizen, thereby granting this court jurisdiction over them. The Slaughter House Cases was the first time the Supreme Court looked at the new 14th Amendment: (Ratified in 1868)

"It is quite clear, then, that there is a citizenship of the United States and a citizenship of a State, which are distinct from each other and which depend upon different characteristics or circumstances of the individual." *The Slaughter House Cases, 83 US 36, 74, (1873)*

"We have in our political system a Government of the United States and a government of each of the several States. Each one of these governments is distinct from the others, and each has its own citizens. . ." *US v Cruikshank, 92 US 542, 549 (1875)*

"The privileges and immunities clause of the

23

Legislative courts are but agencies in drag.
Fourteenth Amendment protects very few rights because it neither incorporates any of the Bill of Rights nor protects all rights of individual citizens.(cite omitted). Instead, this provision protects only those rights peculiar to being a citizen of the federal government; it does not protect those rights which relate to state citizenship." *Jones v. Temmer, 829 F.Supp 1229,1232 (1993)*

I have 15 more citations like these three. You can change your citizenship simply by making an oath to that effect.

Now for the trick: We have already seen how the definitions of the words "State" or "United States" can change. On various State and Federal forms people are asked to swear they are a US citizen. These forms never include the definition of the term. In Nevada, I asked for a definition. This is the (condensed) response letter:

DEAN HELLER
Secretary of State

DALE A. R. ERQUIAGA
Chief Deputy Secretary of State

STATE OF NEVADA

DONALD J. REIS
Deputy Secretary for Securities Regulation

CAROLE LEFCOURTE
Deputy Secretary for Commercial Recordings

JO ANN MALONE
Deputy Secretary for Elections

OFFICE OF THE
SECRETARY OF STATE
September 29, 1995

Dear Mr. Winter:

Thank you for your recent letter regarding voter registration in the State of Nevada. Your interest in Nevada elections is greatly appreciated.

You have requested a definition of "United States Citizen" as it pertains to language on the State of Nevada voter registration application. It is the opinion of this office that United States citizenship as defined in the fourteenth amendment to the United States Constitution, is the intended definition for Nevada's voter registration forms.

Legislative courts are but agencies in drag.

Sincerely,

Dean Heller

By: [signature]
Dale A. R. Erquiaga
Chief Deputy Secretary of State

mjs

In Washington State, voter registrants must sign an oath declaring that they are "a citizen of the United States". *(RCW 29A.08.230)*. In 1999, I asked for their definition of United States and received this response:

Thank you for your letter regarding the definition of "United States" as it applies to the voter registration application form. I believe that your best resource concerning this matter would be the United States Department of State in Washington D.C., as United States citizenship is a federal concept.

I am sorry we can't give you a more definitive answer, however, if you have any questions regarding your citizenship please contact the federal authorities. I have enclosed a copy of the federal code regarding citizenship that you may find of some use.

Sincerely,

Barbara Reeves
Office of the Secretary of State

On the Social Security application form people must declare they are a 'US Citizen".

In the original Social Security Act (1935) the definitions of State and United States, as we have seen before, are:

```
TITLE XI-GENERAL PROVISIONS
DEFINITIONS
```

Legislative courts are but agencies in drag.

```
SECTION 1101. (a) When used in this Act-
(1) The term " State " (except when used in
section 531)includes Alaska, Hawaii, and the
District of Columbia.
(2) The term " United States " when used in a
geographical sense means the States, Alaska,
Hawaii, and the District of Columbia.
```

But when we're talking about citizenship, we are not speaking in a geographical sense. Citizenship is political. *(Baldwin v. Franks, 120 US 656, 662, 1887).* That leaves us the definition of "State" in the original Act. All of those "States" together would be termed the United States. In 1935, Alaska and Hawaii were territories. We have already seen Congress refer to legislative courts as "US" courts; US Tax Court, for example.

 Everyone with a SSN or who is a registered voter has become a Federal citizen. Think of it as being a citizen of the District of Columbia. Now you can be dragged into a Federal legislative court. **Except**, that waivers of rights must be knowing, intelligent, and voluntary. This was stated in the well known Miranda case and it is the standard today. But still, the Courts pretend you voluntarily gave up your Bill of Rights. It's dishonest, but what would you expect from people, like FDR, who are trying to evade the Constitution. Speaking of government forms, the Social Security form, above, has a OMB number in the top, right corner. That means the Office of Management and Budget has reviewed Form 83-I on which an agency certifies the form to be compliant with the Paperwork Reduction Act. (PRA) *(44 USC 3500-3520).*

Legislative courts are but agencies in drag.

19. Certification for Paperwork Reduction Act Submissions

On behalf of this Federal agency, I certify that the collection of information encompassed by this request complies with 5 CFR 1320.9.

Note: The text of 5 CFR 1320.9, and the related provisions of 5 CFR 1320.8(b)(3), appear at the end of the instructions. The certification is to be made with reference to those regulatory provisions as set forth in the instructions.

The following is a summary of the topics, regarding the proposed collection of information, that the certification covers:

(a) It is necessary for the proper performance of agency functions;

(b) It avoids unnecessary duplication;

(c) It reduces burden on small entities;

(d) It uses plain, coherent, and unambiguous terminology that is understandable to respondents;

(e) Its implementation will be consistent and compatible with current reporting and recordkeeping practices;

(f) It indicates the retention period for recordkeeping requirements;

(g) It informs respondents of the information called for under 5 CFR 1320.8(b)(3):

    (i) Why the information is being collected;

    (ii) Use of information;

    (iii) Burden estimate;

    (iv) Nature of response (voluntary, required for a benefit, or mandatory);

    (v) Nature and extent of confidentiality; and

    (vi) Need to display currently valid OMB control number;

(h) It was developed by an office that has planned and allocated resources for the efficient and effective management and use of the information to be collected (see note in Item 19 of the instructions);

(i) It uses effective and efficient statistical survey methodology; and

(j) It makes appropriate use of information technology.

If you are unable to certify compliance with any of these provisions, identify the item below and explain the reason in Item 18 of the Supporting Statement.

Signature of Senior Official or designee	Date

OMB 83-I

02/0-

27

Legislative courts are but agencies in drag.

Let me highlight 2 things that the certification covers:

(d) It uses plain, coherent, and unambiguous terminology that is understandable to respondents;

(g) (iv) Nature of the response (voluntary, required for a benefit, or mandatory)

Clearly, the Social Security form does not use plain language when it talks of US citizenship. Nor does it tell the applicant if the nature of the response is voluntary or mandatory. It is voluntary; no one goes to prison if they don't have a SSN, but getting hired without one would be challenging at best.

FYI- The IRS 1040 Form has an OMB number and a senior IRS official fills out the same form, certifies the same things, and commits the same fraud.

All of this means that the forms do not comply with the Paperwork Reduction Act (PRA) and they display an invalid OMB control number. The PRA protects anyone who does not fill out an invalid form. *(44 USC 3512)*

The Aftermath

Now that the lower Federal courts could not decide a Constitutional issue, they and the Supreme Court could start reversing the precedents set by the earlier Article III courts. Compare the Federal Courts' decisions before 1937, the year of the Court Packing Plan, with those that came later. Along with this, there is a new refusal to interpret words used in the Constitution. This refusal is because the Supreme Court is reviewing the lower Federal courts' decisions, looking for an error of some kind, and there is no error if the lower legislative courts define words to support the will of Congress while, at the same time, ignoring the Constitution, where they cannot decide anything.

1. Income Tax
"The whole (income tax) law was, however , declared unconstitutional on the ground that . . . (it) would leave the burden of the tax to be borne by professions, trades, employments, or vocations, and in that way what was intended as a tax on capital would remain, in substance, a tax on occupations and labor -a result which, it was held *(in Pollock v. Farmers, 158 US 601, 637,)*, could not have been contemplated by Congress." *Brushaber v. Union Pacific RR & Co., 240 US 1, 17, (1920).* *(parenthesis mine)*

and
"At the time of the adoption of the Constitution the term "excise tax" was used only in connection with a tax on goods, merchandise and commodities." *Davis v.*

Legislative courts are but agencies in drag.

Boston MR Co., 89 F. 2ⁿᵈ 368, 373, 1ˢᵗ Cir. (Apr. 14, 1937).

and

"But nowhere do we find that an excise tax has ever been imposed in this country on the natural right to employ labor in manufacturing, or in any trade or calling for profit." *Davis v. Boston MR Co., 89 F. 2ⁿᵈ 368, 376, 1ˢᵗ Cir. (Apr. 14, 1937).*

vs.

"An excise (tax) is not limited to vocations or activities that may be prohibited altogether . . . It extends to vocations or activities pursued as of common right." *Chas. H. Steward Mach. Co. v. Davis, 301 US 548, 580-1, (May 24, 1937)(parenthesis mine)*

and

"The 16th Amendment eliminated the indirect/direct distinction as applied to taxes on income." *US v. Turano, 802 F 2ⁿᵈ 19, 12, 1986)*

2. Defining words to support the will of Congress:

Example #1: the definition of "general welfare".

"Congress cannot by any definition it may adopt conclude the matter, since it cannot by legislation alter the Constitution, from which alone it derives its power to legislate, and within whose limitations alone that power can be lawfully exercised." *Eisner v Macomber, 252 US 189, 206, (1920).*

and

"The proposition, often advanced and as often

discredited, . . . that Congress, entirely apart from those powers delegated by the Constitution, may enact laws to promote the general welfare, have never been accepted but always definitely rejected by this court." *Davis v. Boston MR Co., above, @ 373, (April 14, 1937)*

vs.

"Congress may spend money in aid of the 'general welfare.' . . The line must still be drawn between one welfare and another, between particular and general. . . The discretion, however, is not confided to the courts. The discretion belongs to Congress, . . Nor is the concept of general welfare static. . . .What is critical or urgent changes with the times." *Helvering v. Davis, 301 US 619,640-641, (1937)*

The Appeals Court in Davis v. Boston MR Co. went on to predict:

"If the United States can take control of unemployment insurance and old age assistance by the coercive use of taxation, it can equally take control of education and local health conditions by levying a heavy tax and remitting it in the states which conform their educational system or their health laws to the dictates of a federal board." *Davis v. Boston MR Co., above, @ 377, 1937)*

Example #2: The definition of "Life".
"No person shall be . . .deprived of life, liberty, or property, without due process of law." 5th Amendment

vs.

"We need not resolve the difficult question of when life begins.. . . the judiciary, at this point in the development of man's knowledge, is not in a position to speculate as to the answer." *Roe v. Wade, 410 US 113, 159, (1973)*

In Roe v. Wade, the Supreme Court finds no support for abortion coming from the Founding Fathers. Instead, it relied heavily on the decisions of lower federal courts who found State laws against abortion unconstitutional. The Court in Roe v. Wade, lists 6 US District Court decisions and 2 State decisions; all of them recent, from 1969-1972. In doing so, the Supreme Court is using legislative court decisions to support its own inventions: namely, 1. A Ninth Amendment right to privacy and, 2. the 14th Amendment's right to due process, each of which, the Court decides, includes the right to choose to have an abortion. This is contrary to the primary purpose of the 14th Amendment which was to grant citizenship to the newly freed slaves after the Civil War. Jane Roe, then, must be a 14th Amendment citizen even though she (Norma McCorvey) is white and living in Texas 100 plus years after the Civil War.

3. Jury trials:

The 6th and 7th Amendments guarantee trial by jury for criminal and civil cases, respectively. Juries had 12 members and their verdicts had to be unanimous.

vs.

After 1938, the new Civil Rule 39(c)(1) allowed the judge to try any issue with an advisory jury if there was no right to a jury trial. There is no right to a jury trial in a legislative court so all juries are advisory.

In a civil case, before the matter is handed to a jury an

attorney can file for a Judgment Motion as a Matter of Law, (*Civil Rule 50*), and have the judge decide the case instead of the jury. Or, either attorney can file a motion for a directed verdict. Then the judge can ask the jury to return with a particular verdict. Lastly, after the jury given its verdict and has gone home, either attorney can file a motion asking the Court for a "Judgment Notwithstanding the Verdict (JNOV)". This motion askes the judge to reverse the jury verdict. Verdicts for acquittal are not overturned, but a judge can tilt the field in favor of one side or the other by deciding what evidence to accept.

In a criminal case, the jury verdict is also advice to the judge. Again, the judge can direct the jury's verdict or change the verdict after the jury goes home (*Criminal Rule 29*). And again, how the judge rules on evidence and what arguments he thinks are relevant, can tilt the field in favor of the prosecutor.

After 1970, juries in a State criminal case could be less than12 jurors (Williams v. Florida, 399 US 78, 1970) and their verdicts did not have to be unanimous (Apodoca v Oregon, 406 US 404, 1972), Contrary to the Magna Carta, and the 6th Amendment.

Supreme Court Reversals

From 1810 to 1934, the Supreme Court reversed itself 44 times, about once every 34 months. From 1935 to 2010, it reversed itself 188 times, about once every 4.8 months; 7 times faster. *Source: US Government Printing Office.*

1966 – Murphy Returns

The case Miranda v. Arizona, *394 US 436, (1966),* made a permanent change in Federal and State criminal due process. Everyone knows of their Miranda right to be advised of their right to remain silent, among other rights. The Miranda warning is basically in this form:

MIRANDA WARNING

1. YOU HAVE THE RIGHT TO REMAIN SILENT.
2. ANYTHING YOU SAY CAN AND WILL BE USED AGAINST YOU IN A COURT OF LAW.
3. YOU HAVE THE RIGHT TO TALK TO A LAWYER AND HAVE HIM PRESENT WITH YOU WHILE YOU ARE BEING QUESTIONED.
4. IF YOU CANNOT AFFORD TO HIRE A LAWYER, ONE WILL BE APPOINTED TO REPRESENT YOU BEFORE ANY QUESTIONING IF YOU WISH.
5. YOU CAN DECIDE AT ANY TIME TO EXERCISE THESE RIGHTS AND NOT ANSWER ANY QUESTIONS OR MAKE ANY STATEMENTS.

WAIVER

DO YOU UNDERSTAND EACH OF THESE RIGHTS I HAVE EXPLAINED TO YOU?
HAVING THESE RIGHTS IN MIND, DO YOU WISH TO TALK TO US NOW?

This is an example of the Supreme Court pretending that the Constitution and the Bill of Rights apply in Federal court. But it ends up working against the Federal government. Key are the words: "in a court of law". There is no honest way a US District Court could be called a court of law when the Supreme law of the Land does not apply there. The prisoner becomes the victim of fraud when he is told that he will be taken to a court of law and then is taken to a US District court. Seeing how the Supreme Court likes to quote Sir Coke, this is what Coke said about fraud:

"What otherwise is good and just, if it be sought by force and fraud, becomes bad and unjust." *3 Coke, 78.*

Legislative courts are but agencies in drag.

"There is no crueler tyranny than that which is perpetrated under the shield of law and in the name of justice." *Charles de Montesquieu*

This fraud should render the prosecution null and void and is more evidence that the 6th Amendment right to "be informed of the nature and cause of the accusation against him" or the rest of the Bill of Rights simply does not apply in a Federal court. Does anyone think that the original 13 States would have ratified the Constitution if it allowed a Legislative court, using fraud and deception, to operate in the Several States?

Chapter 9

Recent Second Amendment Cases

After 1937, I was surprised to find that gun rights had not been diminished. In 1939, the Supreme Court did find that short barreled shot guns did not receive 2nd Amendment protection, *US v. Miller, 307 US 174*. Other than that, the Court did not explore the full meaning of the 2nd Amendment until 2008.

In *District of Columbia v. Heller, (554 US 570, 2008)* the Supreme Court analyzed the 2nd Amendment at length and used it to strike down a District of Columbia city ordinance which made it illegal for any homeowner to have a readily available handgun in his home. This was a clear victory for gun rights.

Later, in *McDonald v. City of Chicago*, the Court struck down a similar ordinance. This time, what seemed like a victory for the 2nd Amendment really wasn't. In *McDonald*, although the Court talked about the 2nd Amendment, the decision was really based upon the 14th Amendment.

"We therefore hold that the Due Process Clause of the Fourteenth Amendment incorporates the Second Amendment right recognized in *Heller.*" (*McDonald v. City of Chicago, 561 US ___, majority opinion, slip op. 44 (2010)*

So, the four plaintiffs in *McDonald* must be 14th Amendment citizens. While gun rights activists applaud the decision, I hope they realize that the decision shows how the Federal government has continued to use the

14th Amendment to intrude into the police powers of the States. The police powers of a State are extensive, which means we should expect more Federal control of State matters in the future.

Chapter 10

Drifting down into the States

Although focused on Washington State, this chapter will show that when the Federal judicial trial courts are abolished, State courts can go crazy.

Washington State has followed the Federal model of court change, but with less legal support. Court names are changed along with their jurisdiction. Even though the State Constitution, 1889, requires the existence of Justices of the Peace, no such court now exists in the State.

"Article IV
The Judiciary
Section 1: Judicial power, where vested: The judicial power of the state shall be vested in a supreme court, superior courts, justices of the peace and such inferior courts as the legislature may provide."

The State constitution takes pains to make clear that the word "shall' is mandatory.

"Article I
Section 29 Constitution Mandatory: The provisions of this Constitution are mandatory, unless by express words they are declared to be otherwise."

Even with this iron-clad guarantee, no justice of the peace exists in the State. I wrote a letter to the State Secretary of State, who is the head election official of the State, to ask how I might run for the office of Justice of the Peace; just to see what he would say.

Legislative courts are but agencies in drag.

What follows is a condensed version of his response:

SECRETARY
of STATE
Ralph Munro

ELECTIONS DIVISION
Legislative Building
PO Box 40229
Olympia, WA 98504-0229
360/902-4151
Fax 360/586-5629

June 8, 2000

Dear Mr. Winter,

Thank you for writing and taking an interest in running for political office. During the 1955 legislative session a bill was passed creating a municipal court system in Washington State. This legislation transferred the powers and responsibilities of justices of the peace to the newly created municipal court judges.

Sincerely,

Ralph Munro
Secretary of State

RM:bh

Mr. Munro would have us believe that an act of the State legislature abolished a judicial court and transferred its judicial power to an executive branch "court". What actually happened was from 1955 to 1984 Justice Court co-existed with the municipal courts. It wasn't until 1984 that Justice Court was abolished with the Court Improvement Act, *(Washington Laws 1984, Chapter 258.)*

> Sec. 50. Section 123, chapter 299, Laws of 1961 and RCW 3.70.010 are each amended to read as follows:
> There is established in the state an association, to be known as the Washington state magistrates' association, membership in which shall include all duly elected or appointed and qualified ((inferior court)) judges of courts of limited jurisdiction, including but not limited to ((justices of the peace)) district judges, police court judges and municipal court judges.

This is just one paragraph of the Court Improvement Act. Here, a previous statute is being amended. Words to be eliminated are stricken out and new words are underlined. The changes made here are consistent throughout the Act. This act abolished Justice court, an inferior court, and created non-judicial courts: District court, police court and municipal court. They all were given a new jurisdiction; "a court of limited jurisdiction." These changes should require an amendment to the State constitution; but there is none. These new courts are creations of the State legislature, and cannot rule on a matter concerning the State Constitution. This is comparable with the US District Courts in the Federal government, where the Constitution does not apply.

Complicating this is an unexplained connection between the State of Washington and the Federal government. Here is an excerpt from a transcript in a Washington State Superior court proceeding:

```
22              MR. WINTER:  I need to know that to
23        know the nature and cause of the action.
24              JUDGE BURCHARD:  The nature and cause
25        of the action under Washington U.S., law has been
```

Bartholomew, Moughton & Associates (425-252-7277)
3209 Colby, Suite 105, Everett, WA   98201

```
1    explained to you.
2              MR. WINTER:  No, it hasn't, not the
3    venue and the jurisdiction.
4              JUDGE BURCHARD:  I understand you
5    disagree with me.  You happen to be wrong about this
6    point, but I understand your right to disagree.  Go
7    ahead.  Do you have any other questions?
```

Washington U.S. law" was never explained and, to this day, I don't understand it. The State Court of Appeals did not explain it or say that the judge was crazy. I believe it was a Freudian slip.

Same case, different judge:

```
11              JUDGE HILYER:  I've read your
12       memorandum.  I've heard your opinions.  I don't agree
13       with you and I'm not going to grant you any relief
14       with regard to the basis of the court's jurisdiction.
```

Judges keeping secrets.

It gets even more confusing. Article IV, section 1 of the Washington State Constitution, above, says Superior Court was created by the State Constitution, but Judge John Bridges said differently; he said Superior Court was created by the State Legislature.

```
18       The Okanogan County Superior Court was formed by an
19       act of the legislature and is, in fact, a court of
20       record, a court of jurisdiction; and the court, based
21       on the allegations of the complaint, certainly had
22       both jurisdiction and venue over you, the alleged
```

Everyone in the other 49 States needs to check their State governments for similar changes to their courts.

What follows is an example of a State judge introducing evidence into the civil trial the judge was presiding over.

```
10              Further, the Court, uh, has taken

11              judicial notice of pleadings filed by

12              Mr. Winter in his criminal action in

13              connection with an upcoming restitution

14              hearing. He has filed a document

15              entitled Motion to Deny Restitution.

16              And I am aware that that was signed and

17              dated by Mr. Winter on June 12th 2003.

18              I am aware that that particular hearing

19              is set to be held sometime during the

20              month of July, I believe in front of

21              Judge Bridges, who is a visiting judge

22              from Chelan County.
```

First of all, judicial notice is defined as the court accepting without proof a well-known and undisputed of the fact. For example, "the court took judicial notice that water freezes at 32 degrees Fahrenheit." *(Black's Law Dictionary, 7th abridged edition.)* Judicial notice never applies to arguments made in another, pending case. So, what we have here is Judge Bridges trying to influence another case by delivering paperwork from a case he is hearing. Judge Allen accepts the influence, introduces it into her case by way of judicial notice when what she was really doing was entering evidence. She does this without prior notice to the parties which results in a surprise at trial. Thankfully, there are Rules which prevent any part of this sad story from ever happening; forgive the sarcasm. Crazy courts.

Chapter 11

Law Students

Law students are a target audience of this book because they are yet to be invested in the corruptions detailed in this book. No doubt the literature from your law school promised a first class legal education. That promise falls short if, when students graduate, they have not been taught what is happening in Federal or State courtrooms. Are they taught that US District Court is a legislative court? Are they taught about "Washington US law"? Lastly, are they taught about their own status as 14th Amendment citizens? The misleading literature from the law school amounts to fraud and could be the basis of a suit to recover tuition. The facts are impossible to deny and going to court shouldn't be necessary. Lawyers usually try to solve problems by writing letters. But if that fails, the largest problem to winning a suit would be finding a neutral court and judge. Still, this could be the fastest way to change the law school's curriculum. A jury trial might be the best option, but be wary of jury selection in the State of Washington. Here is an excerpt from a State Habeas Corpus hearing:

```
                                                      12
1              THE DEFENDANT:  But as you were
2        saying, jury selection RCWs start with 2.36.  And one
3        of those says that the Superior Court judge shall
4        ensure the randomness of the selection.  I can't see
5        how you can do that if you don't understand the
6        selection process any better than I do.
```

Legislative courts are but agencies in drag.

```
 7                    JUDGE BRIDGES:  Certainly, that's an

 8         argument, Mr. Winter; but when I look over the names

 9         of the persons who appeared for jury duty the day of

10         your trial, it certainly looks like a random process

11         to me.

12                    THE DEFENDANT:  With ninety-six

13         percent coming from the first half of the alphabet?

14                    JUDGE BRIDGES:  That's right.
```

There's 1 chance in 900 Billion of that happening randomly. Normally, in Statistics, proving a result had less than 1 chance in 20 of happening is evidence of a problem. But it looked random to the judge.

After a person's State remedies are exhausted, the next step is a Federal court. Although the Federal Habeas Corpus was directed to an Article III court, the US District Court heard the petition.

Jurisdictional Statement

A court established by Article III of the Constitution for the United States of America has subject matter jurisdiction to hear this criminal habeas corpus pursuant to Article I I 9 of that constitution. To protect his rights and remedies, Petitioner desires that this petition be heard by an Article III court of Law, not an Article I court. Being a lay person, he does not know what secret procedures or magical words it takes to do that, so he simply states his intent and encloses with this petition a praecipe to Chief Judge Van Sickle to affect that intent.

If the court had been honest, it would have admitted that there was no Article III court in the Federal courthouse and returned the petition to me.

Using many of the same arguments as in the State Habeas Corpus, this is what the Magistrate said about jury selection:

If being convicted by a stacked jury is not prejudicial;

Legislative courts are but agencies in drag.

what is? The State judge's statement about "Washington US law" was deemed just a passing reference.

3　　　As grounds for federal habeas relief, Mr. Winter asserts: (1)
4　trial court failed to state its jurisdiction over Petitioner or define
5　its venue; (2) trial court made a passing reference to "Washington
6　U.S. law"; (3) Petitioner's prosecution violated his constitutional

13　　　After review of Mr. Winter's federal habeas corpus petition, the
14　court finds Mr. Winter's assertions are frivolous.² It is clear from
15　the face of the petition he is not entitled to federal habeas relief.
16　Accordingly, **IT IS RECOMMENDED** the Petition be **DISMISSED with**

1　**prejudice** pursuant to Rule 4, Rules Governing Section 2254 Cases in
2　the United States District Courts.

25　　　**DATED** this 25ᵗʰ day of March 2005.
26
　　　　　　　　　s/ Michael W. Leavitt
27
　　　　　　　　MICHAEL W. LEAVITT
28　　　　　　　UNITED STATES MAGISTRATE JUDGE

REPORT AND RECOMMENDATION -- 4

Is there any doubt that Habeas Corpus is dead?

45

Solutions

On the Federal level, the most important thing would be to release everyone from Federal prison. Unfortunately that amounts to 189,302 people as of this writing. Then, pressure Congress to re-establish Article III courts inferior to the Supreme Court so that the reversals, spoken of in Chapter 7, could themselves be reversed by constitutional courts. Doing that would be an admission by Congress that nobody has been able to assert any defense based upon the Constitution or the Bill of Rights in a Federal court since 1948. The damages are astronomical. In addition to the wrongful incarceration, there's also all of the unconstitutional income tax and Social Security money taken by the Federal government.

After the prisoners have been released, the people responsible for the dishonest system need to held responsible.

TITLE 18, U.S.C., SECTION 242

Whoever, under color of any law, statute, ordinance, regulation, or custom, willfully subjects any person in any State, Territory, Commonwealth, Possession, or District to the deprivation of any rights, privileges, or immunities secured or protected by the Constitution or laws of the United States, ... shall be fined under this title or imprisoned not more than one year, or both; and if bodily injury results from the acts committed in violation of this section or if such acts include the use, attempted use, or threatened use of a dangerous weapon, explosives, or fire, shall be fined

under this title or imprisoned not more than ten years, or both; and if death results from the acts committed in violation of this section or if such acts include kidnaping or an attempt to kidnap, aggravated sexual abuse, or an attempt to commit aggravated sexual abuse, or an attempt to kill, shall be fined under this title, or imprisoned for any term of years or for life, or both, or may be sentenced to death.

To stop Federal prosecutions, Federal defense attorneys should have the defendant sign an affidavit swearing that they never intended to become a 14th Amendment citizen and the alleged crime did not take place in a "State" as defined by FRCrP (1)(9). Also, file a Bill of Particulars with the Prosecutor asking him for the facts that establish jurisdiction and to establish which branch of government US District Court belongs. This should deprive US District Court of subject matter jurisdiction and personal jurisdiction. If the Court keeps moving forward, file a criminal complaint with the FBI. Judicial immunity only applies to judicial judges, not legislative judges. Federal defenders could refuse to represent a defendant. After all, the 6th Amendment right to assistance of counsel only applies in a judicial court, not in an agency proceeding. Or, the Federal public defenders can do nothing and just keep signing their names to the fraud.

Jurors could refuse to convict anyone in protest of the fraud and in defense of Constitutional rights.

The 14th Amendment should be repealed because it is no longer needed and neither is a Federal citizen.

On the Washington State level:
1) Prisoners need to be released and compensated.

Legislative courts are but agencies in drag.

2) Pressure could be applied to the State legislature to re-establish Justices of the Peace.

3) Attorneys of the State could bring complaints against all sitting judges for violating their Attorney's Oath (Admission to Practice Rule 5(e)) with the State Bar Association. No disbarred attorney could remain on the bench. I don't know if this approach has ever been attempted. But see what happens when it isn't. It would be a much needed check and balance and it would help to redeem the integrity of the profession. All it would take would be enough attorneys and the will to put an end to "Washington U.S. law".

4) Jurors can take action to end "Washington US law".

5) As above, 18 USC 242 also applies to State actors.

Up on my little soapbox

Realistically, there's not enough money in the world to repair the damages caused by Congress and the Supreme Court. The People, the States, and the Constitution will survive, but the future of the Federal government is far from certain. The States created the Federal government and they have the power to recreate it. Being older and wiser, now the States could do a better job.

Byron Winter

February 2017
Seattle, USA

Legislative courts are but agencies in drag.

Index and Table of Cases

Alphabetical Index